Y0-BGD-326

DATE DUE

Telecommunications

Careers for Today

Telecommunications

Linda Barrett
Galen Guengerich

Franklin Watts

New York • London • Toronto • Sydney

Developed by: 𝛀 Visual Education Corporation
Princeton, NJ

Cover photograph: Steve Dunwell/The Image Bank

Photo Credits: p. 6 AT&T Archives; p. 10 Spencer Grant/Monkmeyer
Press; p. 13 Larry Dale Gordon/The Image Bank; p.14 David R.
Frazier Photolibrary; p. 16 PhotoEdit; p. 20 David R. Frazier
Photolibrary; p. 26 W. Metzen/H. Armstrong Roberts; p. 30 Tom
Dunham; p. 32 Courtesy of US Sprint/United Telecom; p. 35 Courtesy
of US Sprint/United Telecom; p. 38 David R. Frazier Photolibrary;
p. 41 Sepp Seitz/Woodfin Camp & Associates, Inc.; p. 44 David R.
Frazier Photolibrary; p. 50-David R. Frazier Photolibrary; p. 54
Courtesy of Orbacom Systems, Inc.; p. 56 David R. Frazier
Photolibrary; p. 58 David R. Frazier Photolibrary; p. 62 Bob
Daemmrich; p. 68 Wilson North/International Stock Photo; p. 71 David
R. Frazier Photolibrary; p. 74 Kevin Vandivier/Viesti Associates, Inc.;
p. 78 Dave Schaefer/Monkmeyer Press; p. 80 Michal Heron/Woodfin
Camp & Associates, Inc.

Library of Congress Cataloging-in-Publication Data

Barrett, Linda
Telecommunications / Linda Barrett and Galen Guengerich.
    p.   cm. — (Careers for today)
Includes bibliographical references (p.   ) and index.
Summary: Offers career guidance and details the work, training and
salaries of telecommunication employees such as telephone line
workers and service representatives, radio and television personnel,
and cable TV technicians.
ISBN 0-531-11104-0
1. Telecommunication — Vocational guidance — Juvenile literature.
[1. Telecommunication — Vocational guidance.   2. Vocational
guidance.]
I. Guengerich, Galen.   II. Title.   III. Series.
TK5102.4.B37   1991
384'.023'73—dc20   90-13024 CIP AC

Contents

Introduction

People can do many things. They can play baseball and do math problems. They laugh at jokes and tell tall tales. Some even make speeches and run for president. Yet these activities all depend on the key ability to communicate.

Early means of communication were often slow and troublesome. Smoke signals could be erased by a gust of wind. Messengers might lose their way. But as civilization advanced, so did the means of communication. Telegraph wires replaced the pony express. In time, telephones linked people thousands of miles away from each other. Radio and television brought the world into people's living rooms.

Today, Americans rely on one of the world's most advanced telecommunications systems. Computers, satellites, and fiber-optic cables provide services people only dreamed of a century ago. Over 1.2 million workers are employed by the communications industry. They maintain and improve the system.

This book can help high school students and graduates find out about jobs in telecommunications. The jobs in this field are as varied as the people who fill them. So graduates can follow their special interests and find jobs that are right for them.

Telecommunications Today

The telecommunications field has a wide variety of jobs that may interest graduates, including telephone and PBX operator, telephone service representative, telephone service technician, telephone line worker and cable splicer, telephone central office technician, cable television technician, radio and telegraph operator, merchant marine radio officer, radio and television technician, broadcast maintenance technician, and studio technician.

The future looks bright for high school graduates interested in telecommunications. As the graph shows, more people are employed in some jobs than in others. Also, some jobs are growing faster than others are. It is important to look into a job carefully before making a decision.

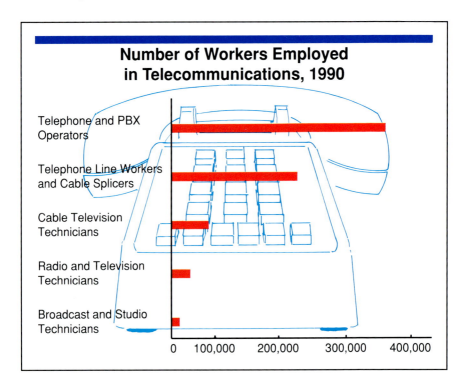

Number of Workers Employed in Telecommunications, 1990

Telephone and PBX Operators

Telephone Line Workers and Cable Splicers

Cable Television Technicians

Radio and Television Technicians

Broadcast and Studio Technicians

0 100,000 200,000 300,000 400,000

Choosing a Career in Telecommunications

The telecommunications industry conveys information in several ways. These include

- Telephone communications
- Radio and telegraph communications
- Radio and television communications

In each of these areas, high school graduates can choose from a number of careers.

Telephone Communications Telephone workers make it possible for people to communicate by telephone. They may

- Help customers place calls and find numbers
- Work at telephone switchboards
- Arrange for changes in telephone service
- Install and maintain telephone cables, amplifiers, and switching equipment
- Install and repair telephone lines in homes and offices
- Install and repair telephone systems for large business customers

Most of these workers are employed by telephone companies. Some operators work for businesses and other organizations. They use a telephone switchboard to connect incoming calls to the right person or office.

Radio and Telegraph Communications
Workers use radio and telegraph equipment to send and receive messages. They work for

- Airlines and aircraft manufacturers
- Railroads

- Police, ambulance, and fire companies
- Commercial communications companies
- Cargo and passenger shipping companies

Radio and telegraph operators have various tasks. Some keep ships at sea in touch with personnel on the shore. Others provide emergency services for people who need immediate help. Still others help organize the movement of trains and airplanes.

Radio and Television Communications

The radio and television industry is an exciting and growing one. Workers in this field

- Install and maintain cables, amplifiers, and converter boxes for cable television
- Set up and operate sound equipment in radio, television, and recording studios
- Maintain and repair broadcast equipment used by radio and television stations
- Repair radios, televisions, videocassette recorders, and compact disc players

Radio and television have become a central part of modern life. It is not difficult to see why. Ninety-eight percent of the homes in this country have at least one television. Ninety-seven percent have a

A technician monitoring equipment in a television station control room

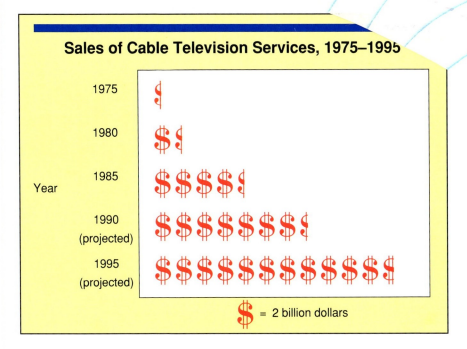

Sales of Cable Television Services, 1975–1995

Year	
1975	$
1980	$$
1985	$$$$$
1990 (projected)	$$$$$$$$
1995 (projected)	$$$$$$$$$$$

$ = 2 billion dollars

color television. About two-thirds of the homes in the United States have two or more televisions. And the average home has five radios.

As the industry has grown, so has the number of workers needed. The cable television industry has been growing especially fast. The graph above shows that this growth will continue.

Many telecommunications companies are very large. Some employ thousands of people. Telecommunications workers may belong to labor unions. Salaries of union workers are usually set by a contract between the union and the employer. Most companies give regular promotions. They usually offer excellent benefits as well. These include paid vacations and holidays, health insurance, and a pension plan.

Preparing for a Career in Telecommunications

People who want a telecommunications job should begin preparing in high school. Each job profile in this book lists courses students should take.

For many jobs, courses in math, physics, electricity, and electronics are helpful. Other useful courses include wood and metal shop, mechanical drawing, speech, English, and typing. Much of the equipment used in the telecommunications industry is controlled by computers. Students who have taken computer courses have an advantage when applying for jobs.

Some people may want to take courses beyond high school. Many vocational and technical schools offer formal programs of study to prepare students for telecommunications careers. These programs may last from several months to two years.

Trends in Telecommunications

Advances in Technology   The telecommunications industry is based on high technology. People used to communicate by sending Morse code over telegraph wires. Then the invention of the telephone allowed people to send voice messages over the wires. Today, new telephone cables are being made of fiberlike glass thread. These fiber-optic cables have a capacity over a hundred thousand times greater than that of wire cables.

New developments in telecommunications will continue. Workers will need training to be able to install, operate, maintain, and repair new types

A cable television service technician testing the system

of equipment. More and more employers will look for people who have had some training at a vocational or technical school.

Home Entertainment Technicians   In the past, radio and television technicians worked mainly on radios and televisions. Many new home entertainment products are now available. These include compact disc players, videocassette recorders, remote control stereo systems, and digital audio tape players. Technicians will need to expand their range of skills. The demand will remain high for technicians who know how to repair these items.

An Exciting Future   The field of telecommunications offers many opportunities for a rewarding career. Students should look at a number of options before making a decision. That way, they can be sure the job is one that fits their interests and abilities.

Chapter 1
Telephone and PBX Operator

Telephone operators work for telephone companies. They help customers place calls and find out telephone numbers. PBX operators work at telephone switchboards. They operate private branch exchange (PBX) systems. These are private telephone networks within a company or organization.

Education, Training, and Salary

Telephone and PBX operators must have a high school education. Employers prefer to hire graduates who have taken courses in speech, typing, business math, and English. These courses make it easier to learn the job.

New operators train for several weeks. They work under the guidance of an experienced operator. During this time, they learn how to use telephone equipment.

Telephone company operators also learn how to handle customer questions, complete calls, respond to emergency calls, and make records for billing. PBX operators learn how to connect incoming calls to the proper persons. They are told how to respond to people who call for information. They may also learn to take messages from callers.

The pay of telephone operators ranges from $14,000 to $23,000 a year. Telephone companies pay more in some areas than in others. Also, most telephone company employees belong to a labor union. Their salaries are usually set by a contract between the union and the telephone company. PBX operators earn between $11,000 and $18,000 a year. Benefits usually include paid vacations and holidays, health insurance, and a pension plan. Workers who belong to a union often get other benefits as well.

Job Description

Telephone company operators work in central telephone offices. They usually sit at computer terminals. Most wear headsets instead of using a normal telephone receiver. This allows them to use both hands to operate the terminal.

A PBX operator at a large office switchboard

Central office operators provide many services to callers. These include

- Helping callers who need the police, the fire department, an ambulance, or other emergency services
- Completing person-to-person and collect calls
- Placing long-distance and international calls for some customers
- Helping customers who have been unable to complete their calls
- Recording information about calls so customers will be billed correctly

Directory assistance operators help people who call to find out a telephone number. Operators ask for the name of the city and the person or company the customer wants to call. They enter the name into a computer terminal. The computer searches its data bank of names and telephone numbers. If it finds the name, a computerized voice reads the number to the customer. If not, the operator may ask the customer for the address or another spelling of the name.

PBX operators usually sit at a telephone switchboard. They may wear a headset or hold a normal telephone receiver. When someone calls the business or organization, they answer the call. Usually they state the company's name. Then the operators transfer the call to the correct person or office.

Sometimes the person being called is out of the office. If so, the operators may take a message. The operators may also answer questions from callers about the company or organization.

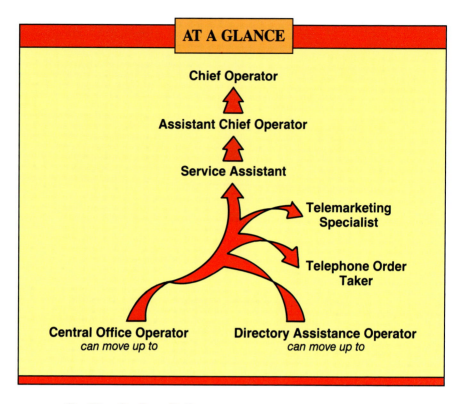

AT A GLANCE

Chief Operator

↑

Assistant Chief Operator

↑

Service Assistant

Telemarketing Specialist

Telephone Order Taker

Central Office Operator
can move up to

Directory Assistance Operator
can move up to

Outlook for Jobs

Telephone and PBX operators are an important part of the communications system. People rely on them to complete calls and answer questions. Operators enjoy talking to a variety of people. They should be friendly and polite at all times.

People interested in becoming operators can often work part-time while still in school. Many businesses hire part-time workers to answer telephones and operate small switchboards. These people have an advantage when they apply for full-time jobs.

Operators can advance as they gain experience. Some central office and directory assistance operators can become service assistants. Experienced assistants may become chief operators. Other telephone operators may move into clerical positions or become sales representatives. PBX operators may become clerical or administrative workers.

In the future, telephone systems will be more automatic. This will affect the number of jobs available for telephone operators. However, telephone companies will still need new operators to serve their customers. Jobs will open up as experienced operators retire or take other positions.

Many PBX operators are also hired to replace workers who retire or take other jobs. Also, new companies need operators to run their PBX systems. These companies will increase the demand for PBX operators. As a result, the job outlook for PBX operators is good.

For more information on telephone and PBX operators, write to:

Communications Workers of America
1925 K Street, NW
Washington, DC 20006
(202) 728–2300

Tele-Communications Association
858 Oak Park Road, Suite 102
Covina, CA 91724–3625
(818) 967–9411

United States Telephone Association
900 Nineteenth Street, NW, Suite 800
Washington, DC 20006
(202) 835–3100

Chapter 2
Telephone Service Representative

Telephone service representatives work for telephone companies. They speak to new customers who call to order telephone service. They also answer current customers' questions about service, charges, and payments. Most service representatives deal only with customers who call about service for their homes. The needs of most business customers are much more complex. These customers usually speak with telephone sales representatives.

Education, Training, and Salary
People who want to become telephone service representatives should have a high school education. Some employers also require typing skills. These skills can be learned by taking typing classes in high school. Students may find speech, psychology, and business classes useful as well.

Telephone companies provide training for new service representatives. The training begins with some classroom study. Then new workers watch how experienced representatives do the job. In the last stage of training, new representatives work under the guidance of experienced workers.

The pay of telephone service representatives ranges from $14,500 to $21,000 a year. Telephone companies pay more in some areas than in others. Also, most telephone company employees belong to a labor union. Their salaries are usually set by a contract between the union and the telephone company. Benefits usually include paid vacations and holidays, health insurance, and a pension plan. Workers who belong to a union often get other benefits as well.

Job Description

When people move into a house or apartment, they usually want to have telephone service. So they call the telephone company. The people they speak to are telephone service representatives.

The representatives ask a number of questions:

- What is the name and address of the person who wants the service?
- Has the customer had telephone service before? If not, the representative may ask the customer to pay a deposit before the new service begins.
- How many telephones will the customer have? The customer may ask the telephone company to install additional jacks.

■ What service options does the customer want? The representatives describe options such as call waiting, call forwarding, and speed dialing. They try to sell these features to the new customer. Some companies offer features at a discount for a trial period.

The representatives make a record of which services the customer chooses. When the order is complete, they send copies to other departments. These include the installation, billing, and directory assistance departments. The installers link the home to the telephone system. The billing department sets up an account. The name and telephone number are added to the directory.

Customers call service representatives for other reasons. They may be moving and want to change or cancel their service. They may want to add new options to their current service. Some people call with questions about their bills.

Representatives use computer terminals to look up customers' records. With these records, they can answer questions quickly. They may explain an item on a customer's bill. If a customer wants a change in service, representatives order the change. Representatives may also suggest that customers buy more optional services.

Sometimes customers call with problems. Some may be upset or angry. Representatives must be patient with these people. They should be friendly and polite at all times. Telephone service representatives spend most of their time on the telephone. They should enjoy talking to a wide variety of people.

My name is Karen Blackwood. What I do for a living makes perfect sense for me. After all, people who work in clothing stores like clothes, right? And people who work for car dealers probably enjoy driving cars. So what do you think people like me who work for the telephone company enjoy doing?

You are right, of course: talking on the telephone! Actually, not everyone who works here talks on the telephone as much as I do. I'm a telephone service representative. I talk on the telephone about—you guessed it—telephones.

People call me for a lot of reasons. Yesterday somebody called who wanted four more phone jacks in his house. He wants one in each room. He said he needs them to plug in the modem on his portable computer. He wants to be able to work in every room in the house.

People also call me when they move. They often want to know if they can keep the same phone number. I tell them it depends on how far away they are moving. As long as they stay in the same exchange area, it's usually no problem to keep the number.

I talk to other telephone company employees as well. Most of the time we talk business. But today someone told me an interesting story. A man called his friend who lived about 100 miles away. His friend answered on the first ring—from just around the block. The man happened to be in town on business. He had had his calls forwarded to his mobile telephone!

Outlook for Jobs

The number of telephone service representatives has declined in recent years. Until the 1970s, everyone rented a telephone from the telephone company. Since then, certain laws have changed. Now people can buy and plug in their own telephones. This change reduced the demand for telephone service representatives.

However, telephone companies are now offering more services. They need representatives to explain and sell these services. They also need more representatives to replace those who advance or take other jobs.

Telephone service representatives can advance as they gain experience. Some become supervisors of a group of representatives. Others become sales analysts and study which services are selling best. Still others become telephone sales representatives. These workers deal with business customers.

Overall, the future for telephone service representatives is fair to good. They develop valuable skills, get excellent benefits, and have many opportunities for advancement.

For more information on telephone service representatives, write to:

Communications Workers of America
1925 K Street, NW
Washington, DC 20006
(202) 728–2300

Tele-Communications Association
858 Oak Park Road, Suite 102
Covina, CA 91724–3625
(818) 967–9411

United States Telephone Association
900 Nineteenth Street, NW, Suite 800
Washington, DC 20006
(202) 835–3100

Chapter 3
Telephone Service Technician

Telephone service technicians work for telephone companies. They install and repair telephone lines and switchboards. Technicians do these jobs in private homes and apartments and in office buildings.

Education, Training, and Salary

Telephone service technicians must have a high school education. Some employers prefer to hire people who have taken electronics courses. These courses are offered by many vocational and technical schools. Employers want technicians who can work well with their hands. They also look for people with good eyesight.

Telephone companies provide on-the-job training for new technicians. The training program lasts for several months. It begins with classroom study. Then technicians help more experienced workers. Technicians who install private branch exchange (PBX) systems need more training. These systems are used by business customers. They are more complex than home systems are.

Telephone service technicians start at a salary of about $15,000. Experienced installers and repairers earn between $28,000 and $33,000 a year.

Telephone companies pay more in some areas than in others. Also, most telephone company employees belong to a labor union. Their salaries are usually set by a contract between the union and the telephone company. Benefits usually include paid vacations and holidays, health insurance, and a pension plan.

Job Description

Telephone service technicians install and maintain telephone wires, switches, and terminal boxes. These link a home or office to the main telephone system. The technicians' work can be divided into four basic jobs. Each technician may do one or more of these jobs.

Telephone Installer   When people buy a new house, they may want more places to plug in their telephones. This can also happen when people move. A small business may hire a new employee. The employee's desk may need a telephone. Or a company may decide to have a pay phone installed in its lobby.

Telephone installers take care of situations like these. Installers put telephone wires, terminal boxes, and jacks in homes and small offices. They may use drills to make holes for wires in walls or floors. Then they use screwdrivers and pliers to connect the wires to jacks. People can plug their telephones into these jacks. When the wires are in place, the technicians connect them to terminal boxes. These boxes link homes to the outside lines.

Telephone Repairer   Sometimes people have problems with their telephone service. If so, the source of the problem must be found. It may be a fault in one of the telephones. Telephones are not usually repaired by the telephone company. However, the problem may be in the wiring. In this case, telephone repairers work with central office technicians to find the problem.

The repairers use a handset to test the wires. If the fault is in the house or office wiring, a telephone repairer fixes it. Repairers also fix public telephones. Central office technicians fix problems in outside wires.

PBX Installer   Small businesses often have simple telephone systems. They may have only one or two incoming lines. Large companies often use dozens or even hundreds of incoming lines. A switchboard connects these lines to individual telephones. The switchboard, telephones, and inside wires make up a PBX system. PBX installers put these systems in offices, stores, and hotels. PBX systems can be very complex. For this reason, PBX installers receive more training than do telephone installers.

PBX installers also install data links. These are telephone lines used by computers and fax machines to transfer data. Some installers set up mobile telephones. They may also install the telephone lines used for radio and television broadcast equipment.

PBX Repairer   PBX repairers are trained to find problems in PBX systems. They use test instruments to locate faults in lines and equipment. Many PBX repairers also install PBX systems and data links.

Outlook for Jobs

Today, most new buildings are prewired for telephone service. However, many people ask the

A PBX repairer locating a fault in the system

telephone company to put in more jacks. Also, the demand for new PBX systems will continue. And telephone and PBX repairers are needed to repair lines and systems that wear out. Most new telephone service technicians will be hired to replace workers who retire or take other jobs. Students who have taken courses in math, electronics, and physics will have an advantage.

Technicians can advance as they gain experience and get more training. Telephone companies usually give regular promotions. Telephone installers and repairers can become PBX installers and repairers. Others become sales representatives or customer service workers.

For more information on telephone service technicians, write to:

Communications Workers of America
1925 K Street, NW
Washington, DC 20006
(202) 728–2300

International Brotherhood of Electrical Workers
1125 Fifteenth Street, NW
Washington, DC 20005
(202) 833–7000

United States Telephone Association
900 Nineteenth Street, NW, Suite 800
Washington, DC 20006
(202) 835–3100

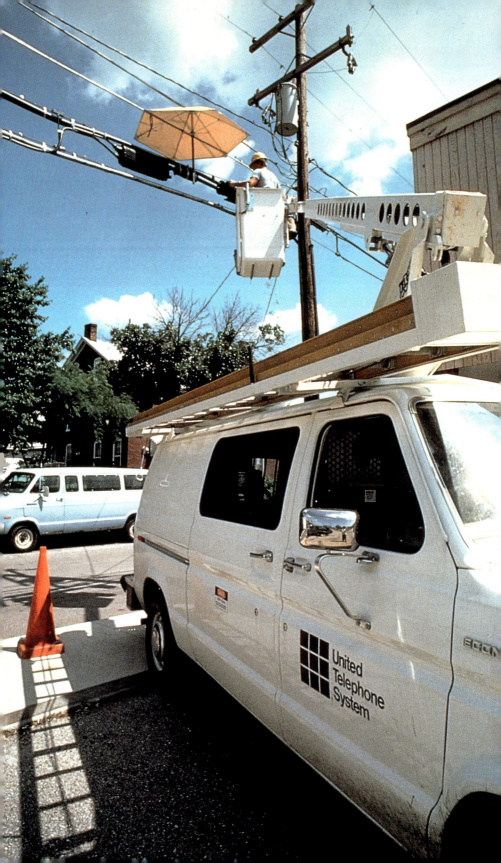

Chapter 4
Telephone Line Worker and Cable Splicer

Telephone line workers and cable splicers work for telephone companies. They install and maintain the 1.3 billion miles of wire in the telephone system. The telephone lines link telephones and private branch exchange (PBX) systems to a central office. There switching equipment completes the connections between callers.

Education, Training, and Salary

Most telephone companies prefer to hire high school graduates. They give applicants tests to measure reading, math, and reasoning skills. The tests often include manual skills. Applicants who do well have a better chance of being hired. Those interested in telephone line and cable work should prepare while in high school.

Students should take as many math and English courses as they can. A course in basic electricity is also helpful. And courses in wood and metal shop can improve manual skills. Applicants must be fit enough to climb poles and lift heavy objects.

Telephone line workers and cable splicers usually train on the job. They may begin with some classroom study. Then they help more experienced workers do their jobs.

The pay of telephone line workers and cable splicers averages $27,000 a year. Experienced workers often earn more than $30,000 a year. Telephone companies pay more in some areas than in others. Also, most telephone company employees belong to a labor union. Their salaries are usually set by a contract between the union and the telephone company. Benefits usually include paid vacations and holidays, health insurance, and a pension plan.

Job Description

Installing and maintaining the network of telephone lines involves several steps. Each step is done by workers who specialize in that task.

Construction Line Installer   These workers install new telephone lines. The lines may connect a new group of houses or offices to existing lines. Or they may improve the telephone service in an area. Installers usually work in groups of two to five people.

In some areas, workers place the lines in underground tunnels. In others, they must put up telephone poles. First, the installers dig a hole. Then they raise the pole into position. Concrete is poured around the pole to keep it in place. Finally, the installers cover the rest of the hole with dirt.

When the poles are secure, installers put telephone equipment in place. They also string telephone cables along the poles. They leave the ends of the cables free for the cable splicers to work on.

Cable Splicer   Cable splicers complete the work begun by the installers. They connect the

A construction line installer connects a new telephone line.

telephone cables to telephone equipment. Splicers must look at diagrams of the telephone circuits. These diagrams show them how to splice the cables.

Around each cable are layers of lead covering and insulation. Splicers cut away these layers. They use test equipment to identify the two ends of each wire in the cable. To join two wires, splicers twist the ends and solder them together. They wrap the soldered connection with insulation. Then they slip a lead sleeve over it. Lead helps protect the telephone circuits from outside interference.

Some new telephone cables are made of fibers of glass. Splicing fiber-optic cables is a delicate task. Often it is done with special equipment.

35

In ancient times, people used fire as a signal. The light from a fire could warn of danger or invite neighbors to a feast. People also created spoken and written languages. They used word of mouth and letters to carry messages.

In recent times, metal wires were used to carry telephone messages. Each wire could carry one message at a time. The wires were joined together to form a telephone cable.

Today, as in ancient times, light is being used to carry messages. People are not building signal fires, of course. Rather, a new kind of cable has been developed. It is made of many tiny threadlike fibers of glass. Pulses of light are sent through these fiber-optic cables.

Fiber optics is a great improvement over wire. Each fiber-optic cable can carry 100,000 times more information than a wire cable can.

Telephone Line Tester, Maintainer, and Repairer   Americans make constant use of their telephones. They count on reliable service. So telephone companies must keep telephone cables and other equipment in top shape.

These jobs are performed by line testers, maintainers, and repairers. Some installers and cable splicers also help maintain the cable system. The workers test telephone circuits to find faults. If they find a problem, they take action to fix it. They may trim trees to keep them from blocking the cables.

These workers are also called upon in emergencies. Thunderstorms, tornadoes, and ice storms may damage telephone poles and cables. If this happens, workers try to repair the damage as quickly as possible.

Outlook for Jobs

Telephone line workers and cable splicers can advance as they gain skill and experience. Some workers become crew supervisors. Others become telephone service technicians or telephone central office technicians. Workers may also move into similar jobs in other fields, such as cable television.

Advances in technology cause constant changes in the telephone industry. New telephone lines often make use of fiber optics and satellite networks. However, current wire cable systems must be maintained and repaired. Line workers and cable splicers will be needed to do these jobs. Most new line workers and cable splicers will be hired to replace workers who retire or take other jobs.

For more information on telephone line workers and cable splicers, write to:

Communications Workers of America
1925 K Street, NW
Washington, DC 20006
(202) 728–2300

International Brotherhood of Electrical Workers
1125 Fifteenth Street, NW
Washington, DC 20005
(202) 833–7000

United States Telephone Association
900 Nineteenth Street, NW, Suite 800
Washington, DC 20006
(202) 835–3100

Chapter 5
Telephone Central Office Technician

Telephone central office technicians install and maintain telephone switching equipment. This equipment automatically connects calls made by telephone customers. These technicians work for telephone companies and telephone equipment manufacturers. Most of their work is done in the central offices of telephone companies.

Education, Training, and Salary

Telephone central office technicians must have a high school education. Students should take as many math and shop courses as they can. Courses in electricity and physics are also useful.

Some employers prefer to hire people who have previous experience or training. Military service is one way to gain a background in electronics. Or high school graduates can take courses in electronics. These courses are offered by many vocational and technical schools.

New technicians employed by telephone companies receive on-the-job training. The training program includes some classroom study. Technicians also work with more experienced workers.

Telephone service technicians start at a salary of about $15,500. Experienced technicians can earn more than $30,000 a year. Some telephone companies and equipment manufacturers pay more than others do. Also, most telephone company employees belong to a labor union. Their salaries are usually set by a contract between the union and the telephone company. Technicians often receive extra pay if they work nights or weekends.

Benefits usually include paid vacations and holidays, health insurance, and a pension plan. Union workers often get other benefits as well.

Job Description

Making a telephone call seems so simple. A caller picks up a telephone and dials a number. Another person answers the telephone. The two people speak to each other. What is so complex about that?

Let's say the person is making a long-distance call. The call is between only two telephones out of over 150 million telephones in this country. Somehow, the telephone company must link the right two telephones. That is where telephone lines and switching equipment come in.

Telephone company computers read the number that has been dialed. Then the switching equipment sends the call over the proper lines to link the two telephones. Central office technicians install and maintain this equipment. Their work can be divided into four basic jobs. Each technician may do one or more of these jobs.

Central Office Installer
These workers install switching equipment in central offices. They use diagrams and other instructions to position the equipment correctly. Then they hook up the electrical equipment that supplies the power.

Finally, they connect the main incoming and outgoing telephone lines to the switching equipment.

Frame Wirer   All telephone calls come into the central office. There they are spread out by passing through frames made of wires and connections. Frame wirers repair and improve this equipment.

First, they disconnect the frames from the main telephone lines. They use soldering irons to take out or add connecting wires. These changes create new circuit patterns. The technicians test the circuits to make sure they work properly. Then they wire the frames back into the telephone network.

Test Desk Technician   Test desk technicians look for trouble in telephone lines. Sometimes problems develop in a line. A wire may have broken. Or a switch may no longer work. Test

A test desk technician testing lines in the central office

desk technicians test the lines to locate the fault. They report what they find. They may also send a maintenance crew to make repairs.

Switching Equipment Technician These workers test and maintain telephone switching equipment. This equipment automatically connects telephone calls. Most of the equipment is electromechanical. That is, it carries electrical signals but works mechanically. Technicians clean the switches. They may replace the contact points and grease the moving parts. Some new switches are fully electronic. They need less maintenance.

Outlook for Jobs

Telephone central office technicians can advance as they gain experience. Telephone companies usually give regular promotions. Some technicians become supervisors. With more training, some become engineering assistants. Technicians may also become administrative staff workers.

The outlook for telephone central office technicians is mixed. The demand for telephone services is increasing. Workers will be needed to install equipment to provide these services. Also, new technicians will be hired to replace workers who retire or take other jobs. However, the use of electronic equipment will reduce the need for workers who maintain equipment.

Telephone central office technicians enjoy a rewarding career. They provide a key service for the telecommunications industry. People who want to enter this industry should plan ahead. Students who have taken courses in math, electronics, and physics have an advantage.

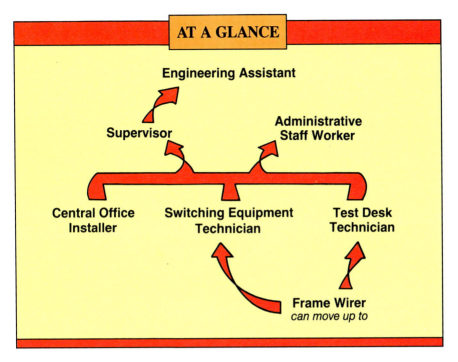

AT A GLANCE

Engineering Assistant

Supervisor

Administrative
Staff Worker

Central Office
Installer

Switching Equipment
Technician

Test Desk
Technician

Frame Wirer
can move up to

For more information on telephone service technicians, write to:

Communications Workers of America
1925 K Street, NW
Washington, DC 20006
(202) 728–2300

International Brotherhood of Electrical Workers
1125 Fifteenth Street, NW
Washington, DC 20005
(202) 833–7000

United States Telephone Association
900 Nineteenth Street, NW, Suite 800
Washington, DC 20006
(202) 835–3100

Chapter 6
Cable Television Technician

Some television signals are broadcast from a transmitter tower. People do not pay to pick up these signals. Other signals are transmitted through a cable. More and more people are paying for cable television service. They do this for two reasons. Cable signals often give a better television picture than broadcast signals do. And cable systems usually offer many more stations than broadcast signals provide. Cable television technicians help make this technology available. They install and maintain cable television equipment.

Education, Training, and Salary

Cable television technicians must have a high school education. Most employers look for people who have taken math and shop courses. Many prefer to hire people with some training in electricity and electronics. Technicians need to know how to

- Maintain and repair electronic equipment
- Wire electrical circuits
- Troubleshoot electronic systems

These skills can be developed on the job. Many cable television companies have training programs for new technicians. These programs may include some classroom study. Most of the training occurs while new technicians are working with an experienced technician.

Many trade schools also train cable television technicians. Programs for installers may last five to seven weeks. They often include some training in customer relations.

Trunk, service, and bench technicians need more training. Most study telecommunications at a technical institute or junior college. The courses of study last from one to two years.

Cable television installers earn an average of $14,500 a year. Trunk, service, and bench technicians average $19,500 a year. Benefits may include paid vacations and holidays, health insurance, and a pension plan. Technicians usually receive extra pay for overtime work.

Job Description

Cable Television Installer   Customers order cable service for their homes, offices, restaurants, or hotels. Installers connect television sets in these places to the main cable system. In some areas, the main trunk lines are strung on telephone poles. In others, the cables are buried underground.

The installers connect a line to the outside trunk line. They run the line into the customer's house. The installers may be able to connect the line directly to the television. However, most cable systems scramble some of their signals. So the installers must connect the drop line to a converter box to unscramble the signals. Then they connect the converter to the television.

Unlike most other cable employees, installers usually have direct contact with cable customers. They may answer questions about the cable service. Sometimes they show customers how to operate a converter box. In some cases, installers refer questions to customer service representatives. Installers should enjoy talking to a wide variety of people. They should be friendly and polite at all times.

Service and Trunk Technician   These technicians take care of the main cable lines, called trunk lines. They check the lines for wear and perform routine maintenance. If a storm or accident damages the lines, technicians replace them. They may also need to replace some of the cable poles.

Sometimes customers report a reception problem. Service and trunk technicians use electronic test equipment to scan the system. With the help of diagrams, they locate the fault. They may have to replace some of the cable lines. Or an amplifier may not be working properly. The technicians may be able to fix the amplifier on the spot. If not, they replace it with another one.

Service and trunk technicians are a key part of the cable system. They try to keep the system in good working order. When possible, they try to prevent interruptions in cable service.

Bench Technicians   Bench technicians do not usually go to homes or work on trunk lines. They do their job at a workbench in the cable company's repair shop. Converter boxes, amplifiers, and other cable equipment often have to be repaired. This work is done by bench technicians.

They usually have more electronics experience than other cable workers have.

Outlook for Jobs

Cable television technicians can advance as they receive more training. Installers who have some training in telecommunications can become service and trunk technicians. Some service and trunk technicians train to become chief cable television technicians. These technicians work

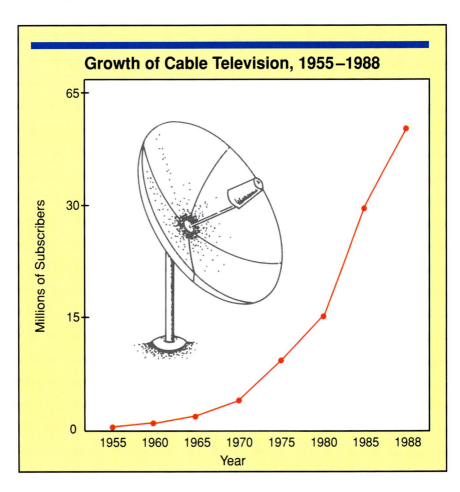

Growth of Cable Television, 1955–1988

with the complex cable antenna systems. The antennas receive signals that are sent to customers over the cable lines. Some cable companies want their chief technicians to have a college degree in electrical engineering.

The cable industry has been growing rapidly. Cable systems have been installed in many areas in recent years. However, some areas still do not have cable service. Demand for installers will be highest in these areas. In other areas, installers will be needed when people move or make changes in their service.

In the future, cable companies will continue to improve the services they offer. They will need service, trunk, and bench technicians to maintain the system that provides these services. The future is bright for technicians who can do these jobs.

For more information on cable television technicians, write to:

Federal Communications Commission
1919 M Street, NW
Washington, DC 20554
(202) 632–7000

National Association of Broadcast Employees and Technicians
7101 Wisconsin Avenue, Suite 800
Bethesda, MD 20814
(301) 657–8420

National Cable Television Association
1724 Massachusetts Avenue, NW
Washington, DC 20036
(202) 775–3550

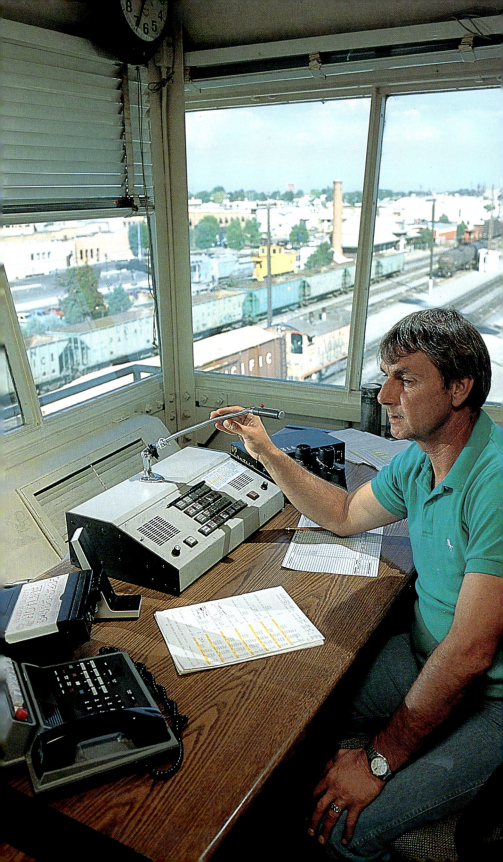

Chapter 7
Radio and Telegraph Operator

Radio and telegraph operators send and receive radio messages. They use radiotelephones and radiotelegraphic equipment to do their jobs. These operators work for

- Airlines and aircraft manufacturers
- Railroads
- Police, ambulance, and fire companies
- Commercial communications companies

Education, Training, and Salary

Radio and telegraph operators must have a high school education. While in high school, future operators should take English, math, speech, and typing. English and speech classes will help students learn to express themselves clearly. This is an important skill for radio operators. Also, most employers hire only operators who can type at least forty words per minute.

People who want to become radio and telegraph operators can take courses after graduating. Many vocational and technical schools offer programs to prepare operators. These programs may last from several weeks to a year.

Every ground radio operator must also have a second- or third-class radio operator's license. These licenses are issued by the Federal Communications Commission (FCC). Applicants take a written exam to test their knowledge of radio equipment and procedures. Some people take a home study course to prepare for the exam.

Employers usually train new radio and telegraph operators on the job. The operators learn their duties by working with experienced operators. Some employers have operators take a test at the end of training. Operators must pass the test before they can work on their own.

The pay of radio and telegraph operators depends on the type of job and employer and the level of experience. Radio operators earn between $15,000 and $24,000 a year. The pay for telegraphers ranges from $16,000 to $23,000 a year. Many radio and telegraph operators belong to a labor union. Their salaries are usually set by a contract between the union and the employer. Benefits usually include paid vacations and holidays, health insurance, and a pension plan. Workers who belong to a union often get other benefits as well. Airline and railroad employees may receive discount travel fares.

Job Description

The exact job of radio and telegraph operators depends on the employer. But all operators' jobs are alike in some ways. Radio operators use and maintain radiotelephone equipment. With this equipment, they send and receive voice messages. Sometimes operators hook up new antennas, receivers, or transmitters. They also link their radio transmitters and receivers to the telephone system. Radio operators make sure their radios are set to the correct frequency. They adjust the volume and other controls so they can hear the messages clearly.

Telegraph operators use and maintain radio-telegraph equipment. This equipment sends and receives messages in the form of signals and codes. Operators set the receiver to the correct frequency. They watch the set for incoming messages. When a signal shows a message is on the way, the operators use a telegraph key to show they are ready to receive. The operators write down the message. They may relay the message to another person by telephone or teletype. The operators also use the telegraph equipment to send messages.

Airline Radio Operator   These operators link airline pilots to staff on the ground. They may notify the pilot of a gate change at the airport. An aircraft captain may call to ask a repair crew to stand by. In this case, the radio operator tells an aircraft maintenance supervisor to alert the crew.

Operators may relay schedules from the flight dispatcher to pilots. The cabin crew may send messages about the number of passengers on board. Or they may ask for medical help for a passenger upon arrival. In each case radio operators make sure the message is given accurately.

Radio Station Operator   These operators work at aircraft factories. They keep radio contact with pilots who are test-flying new airplanes. They also keep in touch with pilots who are delivering airplanes to customers.

Railroad Telegrapher   Telegraphers send messages between railroad dispatchers and train

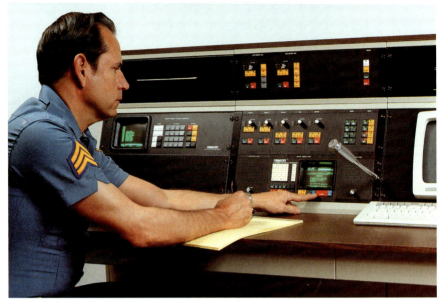

A police radio operator making a call to a police car

crews. Most messages are about the schedules and routes of the trains. Telegraphers use telegraph machines and telephones to convey the messages.

Police, Ambulance, and Fire Company Radio Operator Emergency services must have fast and reliable communications systems. Radio operators link central control stations with mobile emergency units. These units include police cars, fire engines, and ambulances.

Outlook for Jobs
Students who want to learn firsthand about radio communications should look into becoming amateur radio operators. These operators, also known as hams, talk to people all over the

world with their radios. Novice operators can become more familiar with radio equipment and procedures through amateur radio clubs. These clubs are found in many schools and communities. They can also help people prepare for the FCC license exam.

Radio and telegraph operators can advance as they gain experience. Some become supervisors. With more training, others become airline dispatchers, air-traffic controllers, railroad station-masters, or police dispatchers.

The outlook for radio operators is mixed. The number of jobs in the airline and emergency services industries will increase. However, fewer operators will be needed in the railroad industry. New technology may affect the demand for radio operators. Most new operators will be hired to replace workers who retire or take other jobs.

For more information on radio and telegraph operators, write to:

Air Transport Association of America
1709 New York Avenue, NW
Washington, DC 20006–5206

Association of American Railroads
American Railroads Building
50 F Street, NW
Washington, DC 20001
(202) 639–2100

Federal Communications Commission
1919 M Street, NW
Washington, DC 20554
(202) 632–7000

Chapter 8
Merchant Marine Radio Officer

Merchant marine radio officers operate radios aboard ships at sea. Some radio officers work on cargo ships. Others work on ferries, cruise ships, and passenger ships. The radio officers operate radiotelephone and radiotelegraph equipment. They use these radios to send and receive messages, weather reports, and navigational data.

Education, Training, and Salary

People who want to become radio officers must have a high school education. While in school, they should take math, typing, and electronics courses. Taking these courses will make it easier to learn the job.

Every merchant marine radio officer must also have a first- or second-class radio operator's license. These licenses are issued by the Federal Communications Commission (FCC). Applicants take a written exam to test their knowledge of radio equipment and procedures. Some people take a home-study course to prepare for the exam.

Radio officers must also pass a Coast Guard exam. People who have no formal training can take the exam. However, most take a course for radio officers at a state or federal maritime academy. Students in these courses study

- Regulations governing sea communications
- Radio and telephone operating practices
- Direction of message traffic
- Maintenance and repair of radio equipment
- Maintenance of depth-recording and navigational equipment

The pay of merchant marine officers varies with the type of ship. Overall, officers earn between $20,000 and $23,000 a year. They often receive bonuses for working many days in a row while at sea. On the ship, they receive free room and meals. They may also receive many days off at the end of a long voyage. Other benefits often include health insurance and accident benefits. Most radio officers belong to a labor union. Union workers usually get other benefits as well.

A merchant marine radio officer may work on a large cargo ship.

Job Description

A ship at sea needs many kinds of information to operate safely. The ship's captain, navigators, and even passengers rely on merchant marine radio officers to convey this information. These officers operate radios and telephones in the ship's radio room. They relay messages between the ship and offices onshore. They also send and receive messages between the ship and other ships at sea.

Some of these messages concern the ship's route, schedule, and operation. Others convey information about the weather, exact time signals, and navigational hazards. Radio officers pass along world news to the ship's passengers and crew.

Radio officers also monitor emergency frequencies. They listen for calls from ships in trouble. If their own ship is in trouble, they call for help. Radio officers keep a record of all messages they send and receive.

Radio officers also have other duties. They maintain the ship's radios and antennas. They make minor repairs to this equipment. Radio officers also maintain and repair electronic navigation and depth-recording equipment.

Cargo ships usually have one radio officer. Passenger ships have more, depending on the size of the ship. Large passenger ships may carry up to six radio officers.

Outlook for Jobs

The best way to learn about radio communications is to become an amateur radio operator. These operators, also known as hams, use short-

I have been talking on the radio since I was sixteen. I don't mean AM or FM radio. I talk on a shortwave radio. I talk about shipping schedules, port changes, weather reports, and freight manifests. Hi, I'm Tom Harris. In case you haven't guessed, I'm a radio officer on a cargo ship.

The ship's captain often stops by the radio room to check the message traffic. Sometimes I receive news bulletins to pass along to the crew members. They enjoy hearing the latest news from around the world or from back home.

On a recent trip, I heard a ship's call for help over an emergency frequency. The ship had lost power because of engine failure. I notified other ships in the area. I also sent a message to rescue crews. Everything turned out all right. I was glad to have been able to help.

I first learned about shortwave radios when I was nine. That's when my uncle became an amateur radio operator. He would let me sit beside him and change the radio frequency. He became friends with another ham in Australia. They talked on the radio all the time.

In high school, there were three of us in the ham club who studied together. It was easier to learn that way. I took my exam for an amateur radio operator's license when I was sixteen.

wave radios to talk with people all over the world. Many schools and communities have amateur radio clubs. The clubs help members learn about radio equipment and procedures. They can also help people study for the FCC license exam.

Some radio officers take additional training offered by the radio officers' union. This training keeps them up to date on new equipment and procedures. Some radio officers move up by taking jobs on larger ships. However, there is no formal system of advancement for radio officers.

The outlook is very good for people who want to become merchant marine radio officers. The number of jobs will continue to increase. Also, new officers will be needed to replace those who retire or take other jobs.

For more information on merchant marine radio officers, write to:

National Maritime Union of America
360 West Thirty-third Street
New York, NY 10001
(212) 614–6600

Special Industrial Radio Service Association
1100 North Glebe Street, Suite 500
Arlington, VA 22201
(703) 528–5115

U.S. Maritime Association
400 Seventh Street, SW
Washington, DC 20590

Chapter 9
Radio and Television Technician

Radio and television technicians repair radios and televisions. Many technicians work in radio and television repair shops. They may own these shops. Others work for companies that make home entertainment equipment. Still others are employed by stores. Some radio and television technicians also repair other equipment, such as

- Videocassette recorders (VCRs)
- Tape players and recorders
- Compact disc players
- High-fidelity stereo systems

Education, Training, and Salary

Radio and television technicians must have a high school education. Students should take as many math and shop courses as they can. It is also useful to take courses in electronics and physics.

Many vocational schools, technical schools, and junior colleges offer training programs. These may last from one to two years. Students study math, physics, and electronics. They also learn to read diagrams. These diagrams show electrical circuits in radios and televisions. Students also spend time doing actual repair work.

High school graduates can choose to become apprentices. These programs are offered by some employers and labor unions. They involve both classroom study and practical training. It takes three to four years for an apprentice to become a fully trained technician.

Employers often provide some on-the-job training for new technicians. Technicians can also attend seminars to learn how to repair new types of equipment. These seminars may be offered by an employer, a trade association, or a manufacturer.

Some states now require radio and television technicians to be licensed. Applicants must pass a written exam to receive a license. Other states may follow this trend. Be sure to check the current regulations.

Radio and television technicians earn between $12,000 and $19,000 a year. Experienced technicians can earn up to $26,000 a year. Technicians' pay depends on where they work and how much training they have. Those who belong to a labor union often earn more than do those who do not. Benefits usually include paid vacations and holidays, health insurance, and a pension plan. Union workers may get other benefits as well.

Job Description

What does a person do when the television suddenly goes dead? Or the radio will pick up only one station? Or the VCR will play tapes only at high speed backward? For most people, the answer is a radio and television technician.

People usually take a radio or television to a repair shop. However, some televisions and stereos are too large to move easily. If so, technicians may go to a customer's home. They take along any tools and spare parts they may need. The technicians may be able to fix the problem on the spot. If the problem is serious, the technicians may need to take the television back to the shop.

The first thing the technicians do is find the problem. They turn on the radio or television. They look at the picture or listen to the sound. If the set is not adjusted properly, they check the service manual for the correct settings.

Technicians may need to take apart the set and test it further. They use hand tools and testing equipment for this work. The problem may be a faulty circuit. If so, the technician may have to follow a wiring diagram to locate the problem. Or the television tube or a radio transistor may have to be replaced.

Often customers want to know how much the repairs will cost before the work is done. Sometimes it is cheaper to buy a new radio or television than to fix the old one. When the technicians find the problem, they may give the customer an estimate of the repair cost.

The technicians may need to order new parts from the manufacturer. They replace broken parts and solder loose connections. They also clean and adjust the set.

Many technicians also repair other types of home entertainment equipment. The number of VCRs has grown dramatically in recent years. Compact disc players have also become very popular. Customers may bring in this equipment for testing, adjustment, or repair.

Technicians who own their own businesses have other duties as well. They may hire other

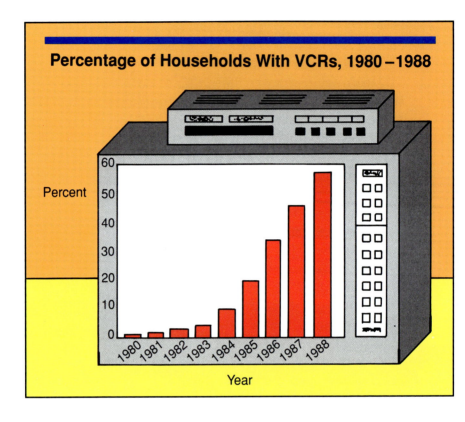

Percentage of Households With VCRs, 1980–1988

Percent

Year

technicians to help them with repairs. They record income and pay bills. Most business owners also spend time looking for new business.

Outlook for Jobs

High school students interested in radio and television repair may be able to begin part-time. Some repair shops may hire students to work at the front counter. These workers may also do simple tasks such as cleaning and adjusting equipment.

Another good way to learn is through hobbies and clubs. Many hobbies involve working with electronics. Some high school clubs build radio sets from kits.

Radio and television technicians can advance as they gain skill and experience. Some move to larger shops. There they may become supervisors or service managers. Some experienced workers open their own shops.

The home electronics business has been growing rapidly. People are buying more compact disc players, digital audio tape players, and high-performance televisions. These all need to be serviced and repaired. The job outlook is good for radio and television technicians. Those who know how to repair new models and equipment will be in greatest demand.

For more information on radio and television technicians, write to:

Electronic Industries Association
2001 Pennsylvania Avenue, NW
Washington, DC 20006
(202) 457–4900

Electronics Technicians Association, International
604 North Jackson
Greencastle, IN 46135
(317) 653–3849

National Electronic Sales and Service Dealers Association
2708 West Berry Street
Fort Worth, TX 76109
(817) 921–9061

Chapter 10

Broadcast Maintenance Technician

Broadcast maintenance technicians work for radio and television stations. They maintain and repair the equipment used to broadcast programs. They also install and adjust new broadcast equipment.

Education, Training, and Salary

Broadcast maintenance technicians must have a high school education. While in high school, students should take classes in math, physics, and computer science. Some high schools offer courses in electronics, radio, or television. These classes are also helpful.

People may want to begin training for the job at a technical school or community college. Some of these schools offer programs for broadcast technicians. Students study electronics and procedures for equipment repair. However, some radio and television stations hire people who have just graduated from high school. They are trained on the job by experienced technicians.

The pay of broadcast maintenance technicians varies widely. Technicians at large stations in major cities earn much more than do those at small stations. Radio broadcast maintenance technicians earn between $15,000 and $34,000 a year. Television technicians earn between $16,000 and $48,000 a year. Many technicians belong to a labor union. Their salaries may be set by a contract between the union and the television or radio station. Benefits usually include paid vacations and holidays, health insurance, and a pension plan. Workers who belong to a union often get other benefits as well.

Job Description

Radio and television studios are full of complex equipment. Sensitive microphones pick up even the slightest sound. Television cameras see the action from many angles. These pictures and sounds run through wires to a control room. There studio technicians balance the sound. Directors choose the camera angles. Finally, the images and sounds are combined to form the final broadcast signal.

Broadcast maintenance technicians take care of cameras, amplifiers, mixers, and other equipment. Much of their work involves testing the equipment. They need to find problems before the problems become serious. Radio and television stations cannot afford to have equipment failures while on the air. Technicians use complex equipment to test each electronic component and circuit. They may check the manufacturers' specifications to make sure the readings are correct.

If they find a problem, the technicians take action. A circuit board may be faulty. Or the technicians may have to replace a switch or control dial. Sometimes the equipment needs to be adjusted. Technicians keep a written record of their testing and repair work.

A broadcast maintenance technician checks equipment in the studio.

Broadcast maintenance technicians also install new equipment. They check the equipment to make sure it works properly. Then they wire it into the broadcast circuits. When it is in place, they test the entire system.

At some stations, broadcast maintenance technicians also work on the equipment that transmits the signal. The transmitter itself may not be at the station. Transmitters are often set up on hills or tall buildings. That way the signal can reach more people. Technicians keep a log of broadcast times. They check the transmitter for problems and make repairs.

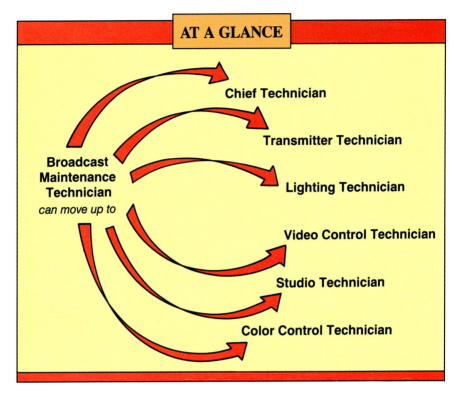

Broadcast Maintenance Technician
can move up to

Chief Technician

Transmitter Technician

Lighting Technician

Video Control Technician

Studio Technician

Color Control Technician

Outlook for Jobs

Radio and television stations can be exciting places to work. Many people apply for jobs at these stations. The competition may be intense. This should not discourage people who want a career as a broadcast maintenance technician. However, it should encourage them to begin preparing early.

In many high schools, students can work with electronic equipment in special-interest clubs. Most high schools present plays. Often, these plays use electronic equipment. Some high schools even have their own studios to record student performances. Future technicians should take advantage of these opportunities.

Students should also look into part-time work. Some small radio and television stations hire students to work in the evenings and on weekends. In this way, students can learn from broadcast maintenance technicians at work.

Broadcast maintenance technicians can advance as they gain experience. Some become chief technicians. Others move to larger radio or television stations. With more training, technicians can take other jobs in radio and television.

The entertainment industry continues to grow. The growth of cable television has been especially strong. This pattern means the demand for broadcast maintenance technicians will increase in the future. Computer-controlled broadcasting will have an impact on the number of jobs. But technicians who prepare carefully can have a bright future.

For more information on studio technicians, write to:

Broadcast Education Association
1771 N Street, NW
Washington, DC 20036
(202) 429–5355

National Association of Broadcast Technicians and Employees
7101 Wisconsin Avenue, Suite 800
Bethesda, MD 20814
(301) 657–8420

National Association of Broadcasters
1771 N Street, NW
Washington, DC 20036
(202) 429–5300

Chapter 11
Studio Technician

Studio technicians work in radio, television, and recording studios. They are responsible for the quality of the sound during studio productions. Sometimes studio technicians are called sound mixers.

Education, Training, and Salary

People who want to be studio technicians must have a high school education. They should take classes in math, physics, and computer science. Some high schools offer courses in electronics, radio, and television.

Employers often prefer to hire new technicians who have studied electronics at a technical school or junior college. These programs involve classroom study and practical experience. Students study electronic circuits and equipment. (See diagrams on p. 77.) They learn how to use test instruments. They also learn how to maintain and repair electronic equipment.

However, some small radio and television stations hire recent high school graduates. These technicians are trained on the job by experienced workers.

Radio studio technicians earn an average of $20,000 a year. Television studio technicians average $25,000 a year. Technicians at large stations in major cities earn much more. Many technicians belong to a labor union. Their salaries may be set by a contract between the union and the television or radio station. Benefits usually include paid vacations and holidays, health insurance, and a pension plan. Workers who belong to a union often get other benefits as well.

Job Description

Studio technicians maintain and operate sound equipment. They may run the sound for a live radio or television broadcast. Or the studio session may be recorded for future use. Before the session, technicians use electronic test equipment to test microphones, mixers, and sound consoles.

Sometimes the technicians need to make minor repairs to the equipment. They may replace a microphone plug or console switch. A microphone wire may have been cut or damaged. Also, the technicians must check the batteries in some microphones.

The technicians work closely with other members of the production team. They find out exactly what will happen during the broadcast. With this information, they put the microphones and amplifiers into position. Then they tell performers, announcers, and musicians which microphones to use. They also explain how loud or soft their voices should be.

During the broadcast, the technicians sit at a sound-mixing console. By turning knobs on the console, they adjust the volume of sound coming from each microphone. They listen carefully to make sure that the sound is balanced. If a microphone is not being used, the technicians turn it

Radio studio technicians operate the equipment that changes the electrical signal from a microphone into signals that can be broadcast over the air.

Microphone Signal

This original microphone signal, pictured here as a wave, is too slow to broadcast over the air. So faster carrier waves are added to the signal.

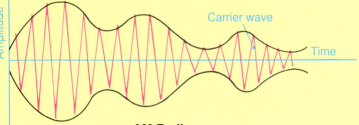

Carrier wave

AM Radio

In AM radio, the carrier wave has a constant speed. Its strength (amplitude) varies to show how the original signal looked.

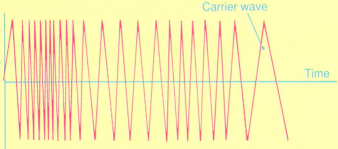

Carrier wave

FM Radio

In FM radio, the carrier wave has a constant strength. Its speed (frequency) varies to represent the original signal.

A radio studio technician sets up the recording equipment before a broadcast.

off. That way, the microphone does not pick up extra noise.

Outlook for Jobs

The entertainment industry is an exciting place to work. Many people apply for jobs at radio, television, and recording studios. The competition for jobs may be intense. This should not discourage people who want this type of career. However, it should encourage them to begin preparing early.

In many high schools, students can work with electronic equipment in special-interest clubs. Most high schools present plays. Often, these plays use sound-amplifying equipment. Some high schools even have their own studios to record performances. Future studio technicians should take advantage of these opportunities.

Part-time work at a radio or television station is an excellent way to gain experience and meet other people in the industry. Some small stations hire students to work in the evenings and on weekends. Students can learn about the job from studio technicians at work.

Studio technicians can advance as they gain experience. Some move to larger radio or television stations. They may become chief technicians or take other jobs in radio and television.

The entertainment industry continues to grow. The growth of cable television has been especially strong. This pattern means the demand for studio technicians will increase in the future. Computer-controlled broadcasting will have an impact on the number of jobs. But studio technicians who prepare carefully can have a bright future.

For more information on studio technicians, write to:

Broadcast Education Association
1771 N Street, NW
Washington, DC 20036
(202) 429–5355

National Association of Broadcast Technicians and Employees
7101 Wisconsin Avenue, Suite 800
Bethesda, MD 20814
(301) 657–8420

National Association of Broadcasters
1771 N Street, NW
Washington, DC 20036
(202) 429–5300

Chapter 12
Getting the Job: Tips for the Reader

Starting Out

Whatever job you decide to go after, you want to do it to the best of your ability. And you can do this only if you have picked a job you enjoy. Be honest with yourself. Begin your job search by understanding your talents and interests.

Rate Your Strengths

Write down a few lines about yourself. Tell what you like and what you dislike. List your favorite subjects at school and your least favorite subjects. Describe what bores you and what interests you most.

Make a chart and list any jobs you have ever had. Include your supervisors' names, your work addresses, and the dates of employment. Now make a list of your hobbies or interests. Also list the schools you have attended and the activities you take part in. This list would include clubs or teams you have joined. If you have done any volunteer work, be sure to list it. Finally, add to your list the names of any awards or prizes you have won.

List Your Job Possibilities

List all the jobs in this book that sound interesting. Look at each job and see if you qualify. If a job you like requires extra training, write that down. Also check the publications in the back of this book. Write down the titles of any books or other materials that will tell you more about the jobs you like.

Look at your job list and your strengths list. See where they match up. Put a star by those jobs that would use your strengths.

Consult Counselors

Talk to a guidance counselor at your school. Ask about jobs that are open in your field of interest. Your state or local employment service can also help you.

CLASSIFIED ADS

SWITCHBOARD OPERATOR Immediate opening. Center-city legal firm. Exp. pfd. but will train. Must have h.s. diploma. $14,500. Excel bnfts. Apply to personnel office, 1221 W. Market, Philadelphia.

TELEVISION NEWS STUDIO Needs studio technician. Some electronics bkgrnd. a must. $16,500, more if exp. 6 & 11 P.M. broadcasts. Send résumé and refs. to Ms. Slade, Channel 7, P.O. Box 1172, Dover.

ALL-CALL TELEPHONE COMPANY Line workers and cable splicers needed. H. S. diploma pfd. Will train. Top pay and bnfts. Apply in person for skills test, 466 Camp, Belmar. For more info, call 555-8900.

Cable Television Installers for new cable system. Start now, earn $13,000 plus overtime, more with electronics bkgrnd. Must have valid driver's lic. and good record. Apply at 100 Alexander daily or call 555-2722, ext. 43.

ATTENTION, Radio and Television Technicians Small repair shop needs technician. Top pay for VCR and CD exp. Will train. Must have h.s. diploma, electronics training pfd. $14,000; $17,000 if exp. Send résumé and refs. to P.O. Box 20, Fort Smith.

TELEPHONE SERVICE REPRESENTATIVE H.S. diploma & 30 wpm typing req. Suburban location. $15,000, excl. bnfts. Apply in person at 400 S. Drexel, Aurora.

Looking for Work

When you have settled on the jobs you would like, start looking for openings. Apply for as many jobs as you can. The more jobs you apply for, the better your chance of finding one.

Research Find out everything you can about jobs you are applying for. Learn about the positions, the employers, and the employers' needs. The more you know, the more impressive you will be in your interview.

Ads There are two types of newspaper classified ads: *help wanted* and *situation wanted.* A help wanted ad is placed by an employer looking to fill a specific job. It tells you the job title, requirements, salary, company, and whom to contact. You may also see a blind ad, one that

ABBREVIATIONS

People who place classified ads often use abbreviations. They want to make their ad as short as possible. Read the classified- ad section in your newspaper to become familiar with abbreviations. Here is a short list to help you now:

excel.	excellent	f.t.		
bnfts.	benefits	or f/t	full-time
exp.	experience	emp.	employment
p.t.		gd.	good
or p/t	part-time	refs.	references
h.s.	high school	ext.	extension
grad.	graduate	req.	required
w.	with	sal.	salary
avail.	available	pfd.	preferred
hr.	hour	wk.	week

does not name the employer. Answer the ad by letter or by phone, as directed in the ad. Follow up within two weeks with another phone call or letter if you have not heard from the employer.

A person looking for work can place a situation wanted ad. This ad tells the kind of work the person is looking for and why he or she qualifies. It also tells when he or she could start working.

Networking   Networking is letting everyone know what jobs you are looking for. Talk to people in your field of interest. Some good leads on jobs can be found this way. Friends and relatives might also be able to help. Follow up on what you learn with a phone call or letter.

Employment Services   Check with your school's placement service for job openings. State and local employment services often have job listings.

Civil Service   Federal, state, and local governments offer many jobs. Find the civil service office near you and ask about openings. See the feature on the top of the next page. It explains more about civil service jobs.

Unions   Find out about labor unions that may be involved with jobs in your field. Check with union locals in your town; you can find phone numbers in the phone book.

Temporary Employment   Working on a temporary basis can lead to other jobs or to part-time or full-time work. Seasonal work is available for many jobs.

84

CIVIL SERVICE

Federal and state governments employ several million workers. In order to get a government job, you must first check with the Federal Job Information Center or a state department of personnel office. Look for an announcement concerning the type of job that interests you. The announcement describes the job. It also lists the education and experience that you will need to qualify for the job.

Once you know about a government job opening, you must fill out an application to take a civil service test. If your application is approved, you must then take and pass the exam. Exams are usually written, but may also be oral. Some exams include essays or performance tests. All exams are tailored to fit a specific job. An exam may cover such items as English usage, reasoning, or clerical or mechanical skills.

Applying in Person

Applying to an employer in person can be a good idea. Call for an appointment. Tell the employer that you would like to have an interview. Some may ask that you send a letter or résumé first.

Sending Letters

Writing letters can also be a good way to ask about jobs. Typed letters are preferred, but neat, handwritten letters are acceptable. Check the Yellow Pages or industry magazines at the public library for addresses. The librarian can help you. Address letters to a company's personnel or human resources department. Send your résumé with the letter. Keep copies of all letters. Follow up in a couple of weeks with another letter.

Résumé

A résumé is a useful one-page outline of information about you. It introduces you to a possible future employer. A résumé should be based on your strengths list. It sums up your education, work history, and skills.

You will enclose your résumé in letters you write to future employers. You also will take it with you to give to your interviewer. Look at the sample résumé on page 87 to see how a typical résumé looks.

Always put your full name, address, and phone number at the top of the résumé. Type the résumé, if possible, or write it by hand neatly. Then state your objective or the job you are applying for. Put down any experience that shows you are a good worker. Volunteer work and part-time jobs tell an employer that you are willing to help out and work hard. Put down your most recent job first.

Finally, include information about your education. You can also list any special skills, awards, or honors you have received.

Writing Letters

When you send your résumé in the mail, always attach a cover letter. Write a short letter, no more than three or four paragraphs. It should come right to the point and lead the employer to your résumé.

Explain what job you are interested in. Include a short listing of your qualifications. Your letter should catch the employer's interest. That way the employer will want to turn to your résumé. See the sample on page 88.

Résumé

Janice L. Hodge
991 Wabash Avenue
Santa Rosa, PA 18452
(717) 555-1522

Objective: To work as a television studio
technician.

Experience

1990   Worked as a messenger at WJZX Radio.

1989–90   In charge of sound equipment for
           spring drama production at Northside
           High School.

1988–90   Sound technician for local pop group
           (occasional).

Training

Basic electricity and physics courses at Northside
  High School.
Electronics course at Willmar Technical Institute.

Education

1990   Graduated from Northside High
           School.

1989–90   Electronics course at Willmar
           Technical Institute.

References available on request.

November 1, 1991
Janice L. Hodge
991 Wabash Avenue
Santa Rosa, PA 18452

Ms. Slade
Channel 7
P.O. Box 1172
Dover, DE 19903

Dear Ms. Slade,

I am answering your advertisement for a studio technician that appeared in the *Daily Chronicle* on October 30.

I have taken an electronics course at Willmar Technical Institute. My experience includes working as a sound technician for a pop group and for a student dramatic production.

My goal is to become a television studio technician. I am currently working as a messenger at a radio station.

I am enclosing my résumé to give you more information about my background. I look forward to hearing from you at your earliest convenience.

Thank you for your time.

Sincerely,

Janice L. Hodge

enclosure

Completing the Application Form

You may have to fill out an application form when applying for a job. (See the sample on pages 90 and 91.) This form asks for your education, experience, work history, and other information.

The employer may mail an application form to you ahead of time. Or, you may be asked to fill out the form when you come for the interview.

Follow the instructions carefully. Print or type information neatly. Neatness tells the employer that you care about your work. It also shows you can organize information and think clearly.

Have all information with you when you arrive. You will need your Social Security number. You may need to list your past jobs. You will have to give the dates you worked, addresses, and phone numbers.

List your most recent jobs first, as you do on your résumé.

However, do not answer any question that you feel invades your privacy. Laws prevent an employer from asking about certain things. These things include race, religion, national origin, age, and marital status. Questions about your family situation, property, car, or arrest record are also not allowed.

The Interview

The way you act in a job interview will tell the employer a lot about you. It can be the biggest single factor that helps an employer decide whether to hire you. An interview is very important. Therefore, you should prepare yourself to make a good impression.

APPLICATION FOR EMPLOYMENT

(Please print or type your answers)

PERSONAL INFORMATION   Date _____

Name _____ Social Security Number _____/ _____/ _____

Address _____
            Street and Number   City   State   Zip Code

Telephone number (_____) _____–_____ (_____) _____–_____
                            day   evening

Job applied for _____ Salary expected $ _____ per _____

How did you learn of this position? _____

Do you want to work _____ Full time or _____ Part time?

Specify preferred days and hours if you answered part time _____

Have you worked for us before? _____ If yes, when? _____

On what date will you be able to start work? _____

Have you ever been convicted of a crime, excluding misdemeanors and summary offenses?

_____ No   _____ Yes

If yes, describe in full _____

Whom should we notify in case of emergency?

Name _____ Relationship _____

Address _____
            Street and number   City   State   Zip Code

Telephone number (_____) _____–_____ (_____) _____–_____
                            day   evening

EDUCATION

Type of School	Name and Address	Years Attended	Graduated	Course or Major
High School			Yes No	
College			Yes No	
Post-graduate			Yes No	
Business or Trade			Yes No	
Military or other			Yes No	

WORK EXPERIENCE (List in order, beginning with most recent job)

Dates From	Dates To	Employer's Name and Address	Rate of Pay Start/Finish	Position Held	Reason for Leaving

ACTIVITIES AND HONORS (List any academic, extracurricular, civic, or other achievements you consider significant.)

_____

_____

PERSONAL REFERENCES

_____

Name and Occupation	Address	Phone Number

_____

_____

_____

PLEASE READ THE FOLLOWING STATEMENTS CAREFULLY AND SIGN BELOW:

The information that I have provided on this application is accurate to the best of my knowledge and is subject to validation. I authorize the schools, persons, current employer, and other organizations or employers named in this application to provide any relevant information that may be required to arrive at an employment decision.

_____   _____
Applicant's Signature   Date

Before you go to the interview, prepare what you will say. Think of why you want the job, your experience, and why you qualify. Learn as much about the job and the company as possible. You can do this through ads, brochures, employees, or your library. This will show that you are interested in the company's needs.

Make a list of questions you have. And try to guess what the interviewer will ask. You may ask if you can work overtime or if you can take courses for more training or education. Bring in any certificates or licenses you may need to show.

Dress neatly and appropriately for the interview. Make sure you know exactly where the interview will take place so you will be on time. Allow extra time to get there in case you are delayed by traffic or for some other reason.

Following Up

After the interview, thank the interviewer for his or her time and shake hands. If the job appeals to you, tell the person that you are interested.

When you get back home, send a letter thanking the interviewer for his or her time. Repeat things that were discussed in the interview. Keep a copy of it and start a file for all future letters.

Think about how you acted in the interview. Did you ask the right questions? Were your answers right? Did you feel you should have done something differently? If so, make notes so you can do better the next time.

If you do not hear from the company in two weeks, write a letter. Tell the interviewer you are still interested in the job. You can also phone to follow up.

Know Your Rights: What Is the Law?

Federal   Under federal law, employers cannot discriminate on the basis of race, religion, sex, national origin, ancestry, or age. People aged forty to seventy are specifically protected against age discrimination. Handicapped workers also are protected. Of course, these laws protect only workers who do their jobs. Employers need not hire workers who are unqualified. And they are free to fire workers who do not perform.

State   Many states have laws against discrimination based on age, handicap, or membership in armed services reserves. Laws differ from state to state. In some states, there can be no enforced retirement age. And some protect people suffering from AIDS.

Applications   When filling out applications, you do not have to answer questions that may invade your privacy. Questions about whether you are married, have children, own property or a car do not have to be answered. Nor do you have to answer questions about an arrest record. An employer may ask, however, if you have ever been convicted of a crime.

At Work   It is against the law for employers to discriminate against workers when setting hours, workplace conditions, salary, hirings, layoffs, firings, or promotions. And no employer can treat a worker unfairly if he or she has filed a discrimination suit or taken other legal action.

Read Your Contract   Read any work contract you are given. Do not sign it until you understand and agree to everything in it. Ask questions if you have them. If you have used an employment agency, find out about fees before you sign a contract. Some agencies will charge you a fee for finding a job. Others charge the employer.

When Discrimination Occurs: What You Can Do

Government Help   Call the Equal Employment Opportunity Commission or the state civil rights commission if you feel you've been discriminated against. If they think you have been unfairly treated, they may take legal action. If you have been unfairly denied a job, you may get it. If you have been unfairly fired, you may get your job back and receive pay that is owed you. Any mention of the actions taken against you may be removed from your work records. To file a lawsuit, you will need a lawyer.

Private Help   Private organizations such as the American Civil Liberties Union (ACLU) and the National Association for the Advancement of Colored People (NAACP) fight against discrimination. They can give you advice.

Sources

General Career Information

Abrams, Kathleen S. *Guide to Careers Without College*. New York: Franklin Watts, 1988.

Career Information Center, 4th ed., 13 vols. Mission Hills, Calif.: Glencoe/Macmillan, 1990.

Dubrovin, Vivian. *Guide to Alternative Education and Training*. New York: Franklin Watts, 1988.

Hopke, William E., editor in chief. *The Encyclopedia of Career and Vocational Guidance*, 7th ed., 3 vols. Chicago: Ferguson, 1987.

Littrell, J. J. *From School to Work*. South Holland, Ill.: Goodheart-Willcox, 1984.

Perry, Robert L. *Guide to Self-Employment*. New York: Franklin Watts, 1989.

Primm, E. Russell III, editor in chief. *Career Discovery Encyclopedia,* 6 vols. Chicago: Ferguson, 1990.

U.S. Government Printing Office. *Occupational Outlook Handbook*. Washington, D.C.: U.S. Government Printing Office, revised biennially.

Telecommunications

Bone, Jan. *Opportunities in Telecommunications*. Lincolnwood, Ill.: National Textbook Company, 1984.

Gould, Jay. *Opportunities in Technical Communications*. Skokie, Ill.: VGM Career Horizons, 1983.

National Cable Television Association. *Careers in Cable*. Washington, D.C.: National Cable Television Association, 1983.

Pearlman, Donn. *Breaking into Broadcasting*. Chicago: Bonus Books, 1986.

Zacharis, John C., et al. *Exploring Careers in Communications and Telecommunications*. New York: Rosen Publishing Group, 1985.

Index